THE WORLD OF ROSAMUNDE PILCHER

EDITED BY SIV BUBLITZ

picture research by Lieva Reunes

St. Martin's Press
New York

A THOMAS DUNNE BOOK.
AN IMPRINT OF ST. MARTIN'S PRESS.

LIBRARY OF CONGRESS CATALOGING-IN-PUBLICATION DATA

PILCHER, ROSAMUNDE.
    THE WORLD OF ROSAMUNDE PILCHER / BY ROSAMUNDE PILCHER.
        P. CM.
    "A THOMAS DUNNE BOOK."
    ISBN 0-312-14771-6 (HARDCOVER)
    1. PILCHER, ROSAMUNDE—HOMES AND HAUNTS—GREAT BRITAIN—PICTORIAL WORKS.   2. CORNWALL (ENGLAND : COUNTY)—PICTORIAL WORKS.   3. HIGHLANDS (SCOTLAND)—PICTORIAL WORKS.   4. LONDON (ENGLAND)—PICTORIAL WORKS.   5. PILCHER, ROSAMUNDE—QUOTATIONS.   I. TITLE.
PR6066.I38Z474   1996
823'.914—DC20
    [B]   96-20046
                                                              CIP

FIRST PUBLISHED IN GERMANY BY ROWOHLT VERLAG GMBH, EINBEK, HAMBURG

FIRST U.S. EDITION: OCTOBER 1996

10   9   8   7   6   5   4   3   2   1

CONTENTS

SCOTLAND

Glasgow○ ○Edinburgh

York
Liverpool○ ○Manchester

○Birmingham

Wales

Essex
CORNWALL Sussex ○LONDON

SUTHERLAND ON THE
EAST COAST OF SCOTLAND

MY SECOND HOME

The past is another country. Dornoch, Sutherland. A village, a town, a city? With less than a thousand inhabitants, yet the proud possessor of an eleventh-century Cathedral, which stands, with its ancient graveyard, in the middle of the main square. To the south lie the Bishop's Palace (now a hotel), the County Hall and the old Town Jail. To the north, runs the High Street, with small shops, and cleft by narrow lanes, brimming with flower-gardens. Once, the Cathedral was Roman Catholic. After the Reformation, it became Episcopalian. Now, it is the Church of Scotland parish church, and filled every Sunday morning.

The village lies on the sea. So far north, the shores are blessed by the Gulf Stream, and the climate is similar to that of Eastbourne. Gardens burgeon with roses, and waves that break onto the beaches are clear as glass, the sands white and clean, unpolluted by plastic or over-spilled oil, and littered only by shells. The golf links run alongside the turfy dunes. Inland, the hills rise, and fold away to the west. Cloud shadows move slowly across their gentle summits and in August they are cloaked in purple heather. The air is pure and sweet as wine, and the skies are a painter's skies, laid on with a wet brush, banks of cumulus revealing glimpses of the still blue of the upper air.

I went first, reluctantly. I did not want to travel to the North of Scotland for a summer holiday, because I wanted to spend the time in Cornwall, where I had been a child, and where my heart still lay. But I had a new baby, and the journey was too long an ordeal for this tiny infant. As well, my husband wanted to play golf. So the entire household, parents, two children, the baby, a Nanny and three dogs, decamped and drove to Dornoch.

The journey took eight hours, (nowadays, it takes three) and it was raining. It rained   7

for two weeks. My husband, golfing, returned each day dripping wet, rosy-cheeked, and entirely happy. Meanwhile I, the children, the Nanny and the dogs, crouched on the sand in the freezing wind, went for sodden walks, took drives into hills which we could not see for mist, and ate our picnics in the car.

At the end of the two weeks, I thankfully packed the suitcases, and resolved never, ever to return. But fate took a hand. My son, who had been three years old at the time of that first, disastrous visit, grew up and married a girl who came from Brora, a few miles north of Dornoch. Her parents were sheep-farmers, and the wedding took place in the local church, with a marquee reception in the garden of the farmhouse. For the occasion, we stayed in Dornoch, at the same hotel.

The weather was beautiful, and for the first time, I actually was able to see the place, and was puzzled by a sense of *déjà vu*, until I realised that it was very nearly a twin of the Cornish village in which I had been brought up. So much was similar. The golf

8

links and the beach; the smell of flowering privet and wild thyme; the profusion of wild flowers which carpeted the sand dunes; the slow pace of life. The past is another country. But it was like going back in time, to days before Cornwall was invaded by tourists and fast-food bars, before the fields around my mother's house were sold for building, and crammed with bijou bungalows.

The years passed. From time to time, we returned to Sutherland, to stay with our daughter-in-law's parents, to fish and walk, and inevitably, for my husband to play golf. We found another hotel, smaller and family-run, perched on the hill above Dornoch, and we filled it with friends. It was much the same as being part of an old-fashioned houseparty, with a severe shortage of bathrooms, and a great deal of delicious, home-cooked food. My bedroom window, curtained in faded chintz, looked out over the first smoking chimneys of Autumn, and the air was sweet with the reek of burning peat. At darkness, the Cathedral became floodlit, like a stage   9 set, and the ancient weathered stone of its walls stood gold against the sapphire sky.

I explored, came to know the little town. The whole place reeked of history, yet everything one needed was within the space of a few hundred yards. A small supermarket, an antique shop, a shop which sold tartans and tweeds; a butcher, a baker, a bookshop, and a useful undertaker with urns in the window, and a discreet notice to say that, as well, he ran a taxi-service. But the best was never having to get into a car, but just to walk across the golf course and down onto the sands, to stroll for miles along the empty shell-strewn beaches.

Gradually, we came to recognise faces, to make new friends, discover old ones. We were entertained, asked for tea, or drinks with the local inhabitants, often driving fifteen or twenty miles for the pleasure of eating hot scones spread with raspberry jam, or downing a dram of pure Malt whisky in the company of the charming folk who have lived in Sutherland forever.

My seduction had begun. A girlfriend had a holiday cottage on the lands of her brother's farm. Visiting her, I expressed a certain envy. To own. To possess. To be able to escape to this empty and peaceful environment. To stop working, stop typing, stop racing around in circles, trying to catch my tail, like a manic dog . . .

She was a practical girl. "I shall," she said, "keep my eyes open. I shall make enquiries. I shall find somewhere for you to buy."

She was as good as her word. Home again, through the letter box came Estate Agents' circulars, filled with the particulars of suitable properties. A croft at the head of a glen. Two rooms, kitchen and bathroom. Beautiful vistas. Needs renovation.

Not for me. Not a five mile drive every time I needed to buy a pint of milk. Not long wet days, imprisoned in a small, dark sitting room, staring out at the driving rain and the hidden hills and suffering from raging claustrophobia. A cottage in the town, then. Bang on the main street, facing north, and with a yard for a garden. But the blurred photograph was not propitious, so that went into the waste paper basket as well.

After a bit, I became discouraged. Perhaps I didn't want a house, after all. Perhaps I didn't want the responsibility of property, the anxiety of leaving it in wintertime, to the nightmare of hard frosts, bursting pipes, and floors ruined by flood. Who would take care of it for me? And how would I manage, returning after months away, to find jackdaws nesting in the chimney and the blankets and cushions eaten to shreds by mice? I became realistic. It had all been a pipe-dream, and perhaps, had better stay that way. But the decision saddened me, because more and more I felt that I belonged in Dornoch. I needed, like some hungry plant, to put down roots, to be part of the soil.

"I have given up the idea of a holiday house," I told my husband, and he looked relieved and went off to play golf. It was the last day of our Autumn holiday and he wanted to waste not a minute of his time. One by one, our friends had already packed their bags and departed, and we were the last to leave. The next day, while my husband settled the bill, I took the dog for a final walk. Across the hotel garden, down the steep lane, and so into the street. Here the faces of the terraced houses were smothered in late roses, and narrow flowerbeds, alongside the pavements, stood crammed with dahlias, in all the garish colours of the Russian Ballet. The leaves on the trees were turning yellow, beginning to drift and flutter down from spreading branches. Around the square I went, past the chemists, the bookshop, the Bank . . .

Outside the Bank I paused, because the dog had disappeared, to chase some exciting smell up an alley. It was a still day. The Autumn sunshine washed the Cathedral with gold. Jackdaws flew around the tower, and a single gull screamed from the roof of the Bank. The Bank was familiar, because it was here that I was in the habit of cashing my cheques. But this was the first occasion that I had taken the time to stand and look at it. I found it pleasing. Set back from the street behind a neat lawn, it had a square

and solid and substantial feel to it, a Victorian building without pretensions. It had clearly been designed, not just for the banking business but, as well, a residence for the Bank Manager and his family. I have always liked Bank Houses. As a child I had enjoyed visiting them, for Christmas parties, or, in the company of my mother, for afternoon tea. Even if situated in the middle of some town, the interiors were invariably charming, with wide staircases and large and beautifully proportioned rooms.

The seagull continued to scream. I looked up to watch it, and saw the sign in the upstairs bay window: FLAT FOR SALE.

Two thoughts instantly occurred to me. That flat would always be warm and dry, because Banks are notoriously over-heated. And no bandit would dare to break in, for fear of every alarm in the place going off.

The dog returned to me. Together we went up the narrow lane alongside the Auto-Teller. There was a gate in the tall drystone wall. I looked over this, and saw the concrete yard, the gimcrack porch set at the back of the house. I saw the spacious walled garden, rising up the slope in terraces. It was overgrown and the lawns were like hayfields.

My garden, I told myself. My front door. My house.

I wanted it. I was terrified that someone else would buy it. Home again, the first thing I did was to telephone the Bank Offices in Edinburgh and ask for particulars. They sent them. The flat was in two storeys, had been newly decorated and newly carpeted. Central heating had recently been installed throughout. There were five bedrooms, a huge sitting room, a fitted kitchen. The asking price was incredibly low. I could scarcely believe my good fortune. But, fearful of disappointment, I insisted to my husband: "There has to be a snag."

"Such as?"

"The decoration will be dreadful. Flowery wallpaper and swirly carpets."

13

"What's wrong with that?"

"We must go and look at it."

"When?"

"Now."

We went. Two days after returning from our holiday we were back in Dornoch with the key to the Bank House. In some trepidation, we opened the front door, and went up the first flight of stairs to the main hall. Shallow stairs, carved pine banisters, pale green carpet, pale walls, lots of white paint, everything clean and new and scrubbed and shining. On the first floor, curved archways led to rooms on the left and the right, and there was sunlight everywhere, flooding in through long sash windows. The sitting room had beautiful mouldings around the ceiling, and the bay window looked straight out, across the street to the Cathedral.

"I shall build a windowseat," I said.

On upstairs again, we found two airy attics, white painted and spacious.

"The grandchildren can sleep here." I knew already where the beds would go, how those children would lie and look out at the Cathedral tower, would hear the gulls crying in the mornings, and the soft thunder of surf, breaking on the beach at flood tide.

So we bought the house, built another bathroom, collected furniture, took possession. The rooms, built for large families, enfolded us, welcomed us, warmed us. In sunlight, we sat in the bay window, at intervals, hanging out, to converse with friends spied on the pavement, to invite them in for a quick cup of coffee or a drink. On cold evenings we lit a fire in the fireplace, dry logs and lumps of peat, and sat in the flamelight with undrawn curtains, because the floodlit walls of the Cathedral were too spectacular to be shut away.

14   We filled the house with guests and grandchildren. The latter needed no chasing to

be out and about, buying sweets at the newsagent, collecting hot rolls from the baker for breakfast, bicycling down to the sands without fear of traffic. My husband, with no trouble at all, became a member of the Golf Club, with its Championship links, and was able to happily entertain all his similarly-addicted friends. I gardened.

And went on gardening. A lot to be seen to, a lot to do. But even the vexing question of help magically resolved itself. Shopping, I met in the supermarket a sweet-faced girl.

"Mrs Pilcher?" A Sutherland voice, soft and gentle as the lands which bred it. "I remember you when you stayed at the hotel. I used to work there."

She was called Ailie. She no longer worked in the hotel, but cleaned the Bank in the evenings.

"Would you look after the Bank House for me?" I asked.

"No trouble at all," she replied, and the next day came with a bundle of pansy plants for my flowerbed.

15

The gardener took a little longer to find, but word went round that I was in need of assistance. Eventually, a young man appeared, to offer his services. He had a lot of wild hair and wore a tee shirt with 'Save The Rain Forest' writ large across his chest.

"Can you start tomorrow?" I asked.

He said no, he couldn't come tomorrow because he was going to Switzerland. Switzerland? He didn't *look* like a dedicated skier.

He explained. It seemed that he played lead guitar and mandolin in a folk group, and that they sometimes gave concerts in Switzerland and Germany. They were a good group and highly thought of. They won prizes for their performances. A musical gardener. I said, faintly, "Well, would you come back from Switzerland and cut my grass?"

He said that he would. So I gave him some money in advance, and we said goodbye. I felt that I had done a good day's work. But when he came back from Switzerland, he went on a bender and was drunk for a week. When my son took his family north for a spell, the garden was in a worse condition than ever, and he and the gardener had a flaming row over the telephone which threatened not only the tenuous relationship but also my property. Finally I rang him up myself. He was charming.

"I want you to cut my grass," I told him.

"Yes, yes," he told me soothingly. "It will be done next week."

"But I'm coming *up* next week and I want it done by *then*. And my husband can't do it, because he's playing golf and I can't do it because I've got a sore leg." (Which was sort of true.)

He was devastated. "And what is wrong with your leg?" he enquired.

So, finally, the grass was cut and the shrubs pruned. The ivy torn from walls and sundry rubbish consigned to a mammoth bonfire. And then, at the very top of the garden, he set up a washing line for me, strung between three sturdy posts.

The sight of this homely contraption, viewed from my kitchen window, filled me with satisfaction. And, on a bright Spring morning, I used it for the first time, unloading the washing machine into a wicker basket, and making my way downstairs, and out into the garden. It was cold, but the first daffodils were beginning to push up through the rough grass; there was the smell of flowering currant and newly turned earth, and somewhere somebody had lighted a bonfire.

Bearing my load, I climbed to the top of the garden, and there paused for a moment to look back. Saw the street, and two shopping ladies pausing to chat; my neighbour was gardening, thinning out his cabbages. I could hear the distant sea, a dog bark, a car start up. From within the Cathedral, the clock struck the hour of eleven, and all the gulls perched upon the tower took off to swoop and glide and scream into the clear air.

I took the first shirt from the basket, shook it free of creases, and pegged it by the

17

tail, on my new washing line. I thought of my mother, teaching me the correct way to do this homely chore. The wind stirred, caught the garment and sent it ballooning.

The past is another country.

Somehow, I had found the way back.

Rosamunde Pilcher

CORNWALL

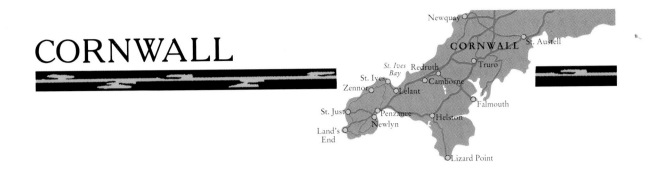

21

ST IVES

1928: Charles Scott and his two daughters, five-year-old Rosamunde (left) and ten-year-old Lalage (right). Rosamunde Pilcher's father was stationed as an Officer of the Royal Navy in Hong Kong and then in Burma. It was recommended that officers should not raise their children in the colonies and Mrs Scott therefore returned together with the young Lalage back to her home to rent a cottage in Cornwall. If she had to bring up her children by herself she wanted to live at least in pleasant surroundings.

Helen Scott was from Scotland and enjoyed the southern, almost Mediterranean atmosphere of Cornwall. She made many friends among painters and authors who had come to live there and was a member of the Arts Club of St Ives. There was plenty of opportunity to encourage her children's artistic talents. Rosamunde Pilcher remembers: "We were always making something, painting or working on a play."

Rosamunde (second left) together with her sister Lalage (second right) and two friends on the beach of St Ives. "Cornwall was like paradise for us children," remarks Rosamunde Pilcher. "There was so much to do: picnics, beach parties, excursions — there was no room for boredom."

1930: Rosamunde (right) and Lalage at St Michael's Mount, Mount's Bay, Penzance.

Rosamunde Pilcher was born on 22 September 1924 in Lelant, a small village on the north coast of Cornwall.

"The Elms", the house in which Rosamunde Pilcher spent her childhood. The huge garden was ideal for playing, dreaming and forgetting everything around you. The ideal environment for a future author: Rosamunde Pilcher was only fifteen when she wrote her first short story.

1940: Once she had left school Rosamunde Pilcher took a secretarial course in a secretarial college that had been relocated to Gloucestershire during the war, learning typing and shorthand. She enjoyed long bicycle tours through the romantic countryside of the Cotswolds and you will find traces of her memories in her novel *The Shell Seekers*.

1939: During the Second World War Commander Scott was relocated to Wales. Rosamunde found it difficult to leave Cornwall, but she liked her new school in Llandaff. "We learned a lot about art and music and were taught choral singing."

Many of the strategically important departments of the Foreign Office were located in Woburn Abbey, Bedfordshire, during the war. Rosamunde Pilcher only worked here for a few months: "I was bored to tears, the work was very administrative and everything had to be kept top secret. One day I simply could not take it any longer. I took some holiday leave, left for Portsmouth and enlisted in the Navy."

Three ladies of the Women's Royal Naval Service to which Rosamunde Pilcher belonged. After two years at HMS *Excellent* in Portsmouth she was sent to Ceylon. This is where she submitted a short story to *Woman and Home* and she received fifteen guineas for its publication in the summer of 1945.

The recruits of the Women's Royal Naval Service had to do mainly secretarial and supply duties, but some girls were qualified in ordnance and learned to handle weapons.

St Ives in 1946: Many young people returned from the war. People celebrated being reunited with friends who had been lost during the long years of the war. During one of these numerous parties Rosamunde Scott met the young Scottish officer, Graham Pilcher, who was staying with relatives while recovering from severe war injuries.

Cornwall also has memories for Graham Pilcher. His grandmother Florence (second right), and her second husband, Thomas Millie Dow (right), lived at Talland House, St Ives, and Graham spent many childhood holidays there. Florence and Tom Dow had met when they were young, and both living in Scotland, but Florence had not been allowed to marry the struggling painter.

Florence was sent to India in 1882, so that she would forget about the unsuitable romance with the young painter. In India, she met and married a Colonial Officer, Robert Pilcher (right). Robert Pilcher died of repetitive fever shortly after the birth of their second child, a little boy called Hope. Florence left Burma and returned to Scotland with Elsie and Hope, and there met again Tom Dow, who had stayed constant for seventeen years. Married, they lived for a while in Italy, and then moved to Cornwall, as did many artists at the turn of the century.

Rosamunde and Graham Pilcher were married in December 1946 in Lelant. Shortly after, they moved to Dundee where Graham was a director of Jute Industries, the family firm. But the connection to Cornwall is still flourishing in the next generation: Rosamunde Pilcher's youngest son Mark is now living at Zennor near St Ives.

Talland House in St Ives, the home of Florence and Tom Dow. Talland was once the home of Virginia Woolf's family. In the foreground is Pietro, the servant the Dows brought back with them from Italy.

She came upon flights of stone steps and unsuspected alleys and followed them down until all at once she turned a corner out at the very edge of the harbour. In a dazzle of sunshine she saw the bright-painted boats, the peacock-green water. Gulls screamed and wheeled overhead, their great wings like white sails against the blue, and everywhere there was activity and bustle.

30

THE EMPTY HOUSE

PREVIOUS PAGES: GODREVY POINT ON THE NORTH COAST OF
CORNWALL

*O*ver the years the Sliding Tackle had remained, stubbornly, itself. Set in the old and unfashionable part of Porthkerris, slap on the harbour, with no space for chi-chi terraces or tea gardens, it had managed to resist the spate of summer tourism which engulfed the rest of the town.

ANOTHER VIEW 31

*I*t was a secret house and, as well, a house that seemed to slumber in the past. Life here, it was clear, had never been anything but quiet and leisurely, lived at a snail's pace; and like a very old and erratic clock, or perhaps a very old and erratic person, it had lost all sense of time. This gentle influence was very strong.   THE SHELL SEEKERS

COTTAGE NEAR CADGWITH

33

CROQUET MALLETS LINED UP IN THE HALL, READY FOR
A GAME, WHEN IT STOPS RAINING

*S*lowly they inspected the house, going from room to room, and Tom's natural interest grew to a sort of amazed admiration, for Kitty had somehow managed to see in a derelict cottage the possibilities of creating a house that was unique. Every room had its charming, unexpected feature.

34 FLOWERS IN THE RAIN

LOVING DETAILS AND
BEAUTIFUL MATERIALS
CREATE THE CHARMING
ATMOSPHERE OF SPARINGLY
DECORATED COTTAGES

35

FOLLOWING PAGES:
TYPICAL COTTAGE KITCHEN
INCLUDING THE AGA

THE TRADITIONAL ENGLISH AFTERNOON TEA INCLUDES SANDWICHES AND
CAKES. A "CREAM TEA" CONSISTS OF SCONES, CREAM AND JAM

She found a cloth and laid the tea, setting out cakes and biscuits, sugar bowl and silver milk jug. Even for kitchen tea, it appeared, her standards were meticulous.

THE DAY OF THE STORM

TEACAKES FROM ROSAMUNDE PILCHER'S RECIPE BOOK

SCONES

The lightest scones are made from plain flour and a quick acting raising agent (bicarbonate of soda and cream of tartar).

Makes 9–12 scones:
8 oz plain flour
1/2 level teaspoon salt
1 level teaspoon bicarbonate of soda
2 level teaspoons cream of tartar
1 1/2 oz butter
1 1/2 oz castor sugar
1 egg made up to 1/4 pint with the milk (measure if possible, otherwise add approximately 4 tablespoons)

Into a large mixing basin sift together the flour, salt, bicarbonate of soda and cream of tartar. Rub in the butter and stir in the sugar. Lightly mix the egg and milk and pour all at once into the centre of the dry ingredients.

Using the blade of a knife, or a fork, mix quickly to a dough. It should be soft but not sticky. Turn out on to a lightly floured working surface and pat or roll out to a thickness no less than 1/2 inch – never roll scone dough too thinly. Cut into squares with a floured sharp knife. Or stamp out rounds with a 2-inch cutter, flouring the cutter each time you use it. You should get about 9–12 scones, depending on the thickness of the dough – use up all the trimmings.

Place scones not too closely on a floured baking tray and sprinkle with extra flour. Place near the top of a hot oven (Gas Mark 7/220°C/425°F) and bake for 10 minutes or until risen and brown. The sides should feel springy when pressed.

TREACLE TART (SYRUP TART)

Rich short pastry:
1/2 lb. flour
6 oz. butter
1 egg yolk
1/2 teaspoon castor sugar
1 teaspoon lemon juice
Filling: 1 lb. jar golden syrup
1/2 pint soft breadcrumbs
3 teaspoons lemon juice

Sift the flour with the sugar, rub in the butter and bind with the beaten egg yolk. Add the lemon juice and about 3 tablespoons of iced water. Roll out to 1/4 in. thickness and line a 12 in. flan tin.

Heat the syrup until runny in a small pan or double boiler. Stir in breadcrumbs until a good thick consistency is reached. Sharpen flavour with lemon juice. Pour the filling into the pastry base and bake for 30 minutes at Gas Mark 4/180°C/350°F. Serve with a large bowl of lightly whipped or clotted cream. Serves 10–12.

MARK PILCHER'S CARAMEL CAKE

1/2 lb of plain chocolate
2 oz butter
2 teaspoons syrup
1 small tin of condensed milk

Warm up, melt and mix ingredients together. Mix in 1/2 lb of crushed, dry biscuits. Pour mixture on a greased baking tray. Let mixture cool down.

*I*t was a secret house, tricky to locate, buried deep in a remote and inaccessible corner of the country that had not changed, either its ways or its appearance, for centuries. From the road it was invisible, protected from all eyes by woods and a rutted driveway, bordered by high banks of hydrangea. In front of the house, the garden, half-wild and half-cultivated, sloped in a series of lawns and terraces down to the shores of a winding, wooded tidal creek.

THE SHELL SEEKERS

*A*nd she remembered coming for the first time, in Diana's Bentley, and seeing the house and the gardens and the distant sea, and being instantly captivated, falling in love. And she knew that she would come back, but knew too that Nancherrow as she had known it would never, ever, be quite the same again.

COMING HOME

COUNTRY HOUSE NEAR FOWEY ON THE
SOUTH COAST OF CORNWALL

FIVE HUNDRED YEARS AFTER
THE WAR OF THE ROSES RED
(JAMES MASON) IS BLOSSOMING
PEACEFULLY NEXT TO WHITE
(ALBA CELESTIAL)

44

SECLUDED BY HIGH WALLS
YOU WILL DISCOVER CORNWALL'S
MAGIC GARDENS

PREVIOUS PAGES:
SUMMER IN A GARDEN NEAR GERMOE

THE ROSE WHOSE
SCENT FILLS A WHOLE WORLD:
ROSA MUNDI

YOU WILL FIND BOTH
CULTIVATED AND WILD
FLOWERS IN THE
GARDENS OF
CORNWALL

45

*F*ollowing Loveday, stepping out of doors through the French windows of the drawing-room, Judith was dazzled by light. The garden was drowned in it; by a glare that the noonday sun drew and reflected from the sea, so that everything shimmered, flickered, shifted in the summer breeze. The restless leaves of the eucalyptus shivered and turned, silver and green; deep-pink petals, dropping from an overblown rose, were chased across the lawn. . . .
                                                                                    COMING HOME

46

ROSAMUNDE PILCHER AND THE SEA - A PASSION THAT STARTED IN HER CHILDHOOD

*A*t this point the coast seemed to fling itself out into a jagged headland, composed of great granite outcrops. Between these the turf was smooth and very green, stained with patches of purple-belled heather, and the path wound down between these outcrops and as they followed its convolutions, a little cove, sheltered and enclosed, gradually revealed itself, far below.　　　　　　　　　　　　　　　　　　　　　　　　　THE EMPTY HOUSE

*A*nd Gus looked, and saw the dark-turquoise sea, the scrap of beach, and the mammoth breakers hurling themselves against the rocks at the foot of the cliffs. Surf sizzled like soapy foam and spray, in rainbow-shot explosions of water, sprang twenty feet or more into the air. It was all very invigorating and very spectacular.　　　　　COMING HOME

LAND'S END (THE FURTHEST WESTERN PART OF CORNWALL)

51

*A*nd Eliot said that if I stayed in Cornwall, he would borrow a boat and teach me to sail; we would go mackerel fishing from Porthkerris – in the summer he would show me all the tiny coves and secret places which the tourists never found.

THE DAY OF THE STORM

NORMAN GARSTIN
"THE RAIN IT RAINETH EVERY DAY"
(1889)

56

*I*t was during her pregnancy that they first travelled to Cornwall. They ended up in Porthkerris, which had already been discovered by painters from all over the country, and where many of Lawrence's contemporaries had settled. The first thing they did was to rent the net loft that was to become his studio, and here, for two long winter months, they lived, camping in fearful discomfort and total happiness. Then Carn Cottage came on the market, and Lawrence, with a good commission under his belt, put in an offer and bought the place. Penelope was born at Carn Cottage and they spent every summer there. THE SHELL SEEKERS

LAURA KNIGHT
"AT THE EDGE OF THE CLIFF"
(CIRCA 1915)

"*L*aura Knight. What a particular beauty that is."
"And unusual. I always associate her with circuses."
"That was done at Porthcurno." THE SHELL SEEKERS

She had paused, turned away from him, as though reluctant to leave the cliffs and the gulls and the tempestuous sea, and return to reality. And in that moment, Gus saw, not Loveday, but the Laura Knight girl, the picture that he had stealthily removed, so long ago, from the pages of *The Studio*. Even her clothes, the worn tennis shoes, the striped cotton skirt, the aged cricket sweater (rather charmingly stained with raspberry juice) were the same. Only the hair was different. No russet plait lying like a heavy rope over one shoulder. Instead Loveday's chrysanthemum mop of dark, shining curls, ruffled by the wind.

COMING HOME

JOHN LAMORNA BIRCH,
"THE SERPENTINE QUARRY NEAR
MULLION, CORNWALL" (CIRCA 1920)

NORMAN GARSTIN, "VIEW
OF MOUNTS BAY FROM
NEWLYN HARBOUR" (1893)

LOUIS GRIER,
"SEASCAPE" (CIRCA 1910)

"Well, then he came back for good. And built the studio. That was when he was painting at his best. Lovely stuff he did then, great seascapes, so cold and bright you could smell the wind, feel the salt on your lips."　　　　　　　THE DAY OF THE STORM

59

THOMAS MILLIE DOW,
"TULIPS" (CIRCA 1910)

JOHN LAMORNA BIRCH,
"THE COTTAGE GARDEN"
(DETAIL, 1897)

"*T*o form a nucleus of a rare collection, we all donated a favourite work. See." He leaned back, and used his stick as a pointer. "Stanhope Forbes." His stick moved on. "Lamorna Birch. Munnings. Montague Dawson. Thomas Millie Dow. Russell Flint..."

60

THE SHELL SEEKERS

PETER WARD, "ST IVES ELEMENTS NO 8" (1984)

"*B*ecause, one day, they will come. As we came. Young men with bright visions and deep perceptions and tremendous talent. They will come, not to paint the bay and the sea and the boats and the moors, but the warmth of the sun and the colour of the wind. A whole new concept. Such stimulation. Such vitality. Marvellous."

THE SHELL SEEKERS　　61

She gazed at the sea, trying to decide how, if she were Papa, she would endeavour to paint it. For, although it was blue, it was a blue made up of a thousand different hues. Over sand, shallow and translucent, it was jade-green, streaked with aquamarine. Over rocks and seaweed, it darkened to indigo. Far out, where a small fishing boat bucketed its way across the waves, it became a deep Prussian blue. There was little wind, but the ocean lived and breathed; swelled in from distant depths, formed waves. The sunlight, shining through these as they curved to break, transformed them to moving sculptures of green glass. And, finally, all was drowned in light, that unique suffused brilliance that had first brought the painters to Cornwall, and had driven the French Impressionists into a passion of creativity. THE SHELL SEEKERS

VIEW FROM HAYLE TOWANS
OF GODREVY LIGHTHOUSE

65

FOLLOWING PAGES:
BUDE BAY ON THE NORTH
COAST OF CORNWALL

*B*eyond Mr Williams, a great picture-window framed, like some lovely painting, the whole jumbled, charming panorama of the old part of the town. Roofs of houses, faded slate and white-washed chimneys, tumbled without pattern or order down the hill. Beyond the roofs and far below them was the harbour, at full tide and sparkling with sunshine. The air was clamorous with the sound of gulls, the sky patterned with their great gliding wings and as Virginia stood there, the church bells from the Norman tower struck up a simple carillon.   THE EMPTY HOUSE

73

FOLLOWING PAGES:
LOOE HARBOUR

THE LITTLE TRAIN ALONG THE
COAST RUNS BETWEEN ST ERTH
AND ST IVES

And yet the bay sparkled in sunshine, just the way it had always done, and the air was filled with the scream of gulls and the strong tang of sea-wrack. Athena was there, waiting for her. Standing on the platform, and instantly visible with her blonde hair blowing in the breeze.

COMING HOME

The smaller train waited on the single line branch track that ran round the coast to Porthkerris. It was impossible not to feel excited as familiar landmarks loomed up through the darkness, and were recognised, and then fled past. There were only two small halts before Porthkerris and then, at last, the steep cutting which in spring was quilted in primroses, and then the tunnel, and then the sea was below them, dark as ink, the tide out, the wet sands like satin.

ANOTHER VIEW

LELANT STATION IS
DIRECTLY BELOW THE
GARDENS OF ROSAMUNDE
PILCHER'S FIRST HOME

77

*F*or years she had kept Carn Cottage, refusing to sell the house, refusing to admit to herself that she would never go back. For years, through an agent, it had been let to a variety of tenants, and all this time she'd told herself that one day, sometime, she would return. She would take the children and show them the square white house on the hill with its secret high-hedged garden and the view of the bay and the lighthouse.

THE SHELL SEEKERS

LIZARD PENINSULA COTTAGE
NEAR CHURCH COVE

80

IN MANY COTTAGES
THE KITCHEN LEADS
DIRECTLY TO THE HERB
AND FRUIT GARDEN

I have always thought that you don't know a man until you have seen his home, his books, his pictures, the way he fixes his furniture.   THE END OF SUMMER   81

FOLLOWING PAGES:
CAPE CORNWALL ON THE
WEST COAST

LONDON

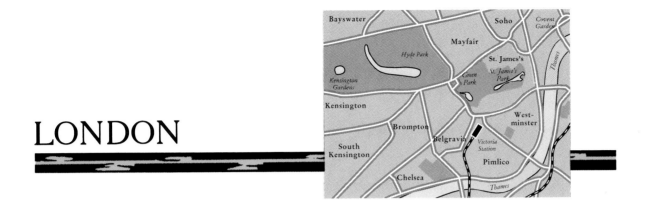

LONDON'S MOST TRADITIONAL DEPARTMENT STORE:
HARRODS IN KNIGHTSBRIDGE

"*T*ell me about the house in London."

"Oh, Henry, do you not weary of all these old tales?"

"I like hearing about the house."

"All right. It was in Kensington, in a row. Very tall and thin, and what a work. The kitchens in the basement and the nurseries right up at the top of the house. It seemed to me that I never stopped climbing stairs."   SEPTEMBER

Shopping in Harrods did not, in Rupert's book, count as shopping. In other stores, he was inclined to feel a bit lost, demeaned or embarrassed, but buying things in Harrods was like spending money in a splendidly exclusive and reassuringly familiar gentleman's club, and so, enjoyable.   COMING HOME

LUXURY ON A SMALL SCALE:
TERRACED HOUSE IN KENSINGTON

*L*ady Keile reached the top of the stairs, crossed the small landing and went in through the drawing-room door and Virginia followed her, and, despite her anxiety of mind, was struck, as always, by the timeless beauty of the room, the perfect proportions of the long windows which faced out over the street, open today, the fine net curtains stirring. There were long mirrors, filling the room with reflected light and these gave back images of highly polished antique furniture, tall cabinets of blue and white Meissen plates, and the flowers with which Lady Keile had always surrounded herself.

THE EMPTY HOUSE

DRAWING-ROOM IN A TOWN HOUSE IN
BEDFORD GARDENS, KENSINGTON

*H*e went to the window and looked down into the garden — a small paved courtyard, with roses climbing the brick wall and a raised bed of wallflowers. There was a white wrought-iron table with four matching chairs, conjuring up visions of alfresco meals, summer supper parties, cool wine.

SEPTEMBER

A BEAUTIFUL GARDEN IN THE HEART OF CHELSEA

But his social life was a different matter altogether, and here he was thrown back on his own resources. Which were, fortunately, legion. He was tall, good-looking, clever at games, and even as a boy had learned to cultivate a sincere and open manner that swiftly disarmed. He knew how to be charming to older women, to be discreetly respectful of older men, and, with the patience and cunning of a well-trained spy, infiltrated with little difficulty the upper circles of London society. For years he had been on the Dowagers' lists of suitable young men for Debutante dances, and during the Season he scarcely slept, returning from some ball in the early sunlight of a summer dawn, stripping off his tails and his starched shirt, taking a shower, and going to work. Weekends saw him at Henley, or Cowes, or Ascot. He was invited to ski in Davos, fish in Sutherland, and every now and then his handsome face appeared in the glossy pages of Harpers & Queen, 'enjoying a joke with his hostess.'   THE SHELL SEEKERS

ONE OF THE MAIN SOCIAL EVENTS OF THE SEASON
IS HENLEY ROYAL REGATTA IN EARLY
SUMMER. EVER SINCE 1839 ENGLAND'S
BEST ROWING TEAMS HAVE COMPETED EVERY
YEAR IN THIS SMALL VILLAGE ON THE THAMES
(TOP AND BOTTOM RIGHT). ROYAL ASCOT, AND THE GENTLEMAN IS
FOLLOWING BOTH THE HORSES AND THE LADIES IN THEIR EXTRAVAGANT
HATS (BOTTOM LEFT)

93

FOLLOWING PAGES:
OASIS OF PEACE IN THE HEART OF THE
CAPITAL: HYDE PARK ON A SUMMER'S
EVENING

96

*H*e spun the door for her, and Selina was injected into the warm, expensive interior of the hotel. There was the smell of fresh cigars, of warm delicious food, of flowers and scent. Elegant little parties of people sat about in groups, and Selina felt wind-blown and untidy.

SLEEPING TIGER

*L*ondon was glamour, excitement, old friends, shops, theatres, galleries, music. Dining at the Berkeley and the Ritz, motoring down to Ascot for Gold Cup Day; lunching in clandestine fashion at The White Tower with some other woman's husband, or dancing the small hours away at the Mirabelle, the Bagatelle, or the Four Hundred.

COMING HOME

One of the delights of the big old house in Milton Gardens was living there in the summer. At the end of a warm and stuffy June day, and after the frustrations of a snail's-pace, petrol-laden journey back down the Kensington High Street, it was a positive physical pleasure to come in through the front door and slam it with happy finality behind you. The house always felt cool. It smelt of flowers and wax-polish, and in June the chestnut trees were out and so thick with leaves and pink and white blossom that the surrounding terraces of houses were shrouded from sight, sounds of all traffic were muffled, and only the occasional aeroplane, passing overhead, broke the evening calm.

ANOTHER VIEW

SCOTLAND

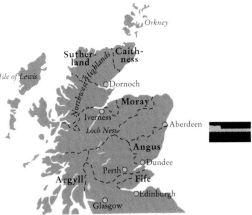

101

COTTAGE NEAR DUMFRIES
IN THE SOUTH OF SCOTLAND

Graham and Rosamunde Pilcher lived first at The Gows, near Dundee, which had been Graham's family home. She remembers: "It was an enormous Victorian fourteen bedroom villa without central heating." All four of her children were born here (left to right: Mark, Robin, Fiona and Philippa), and this is where Rosamunde Pilcher started to write again.

Rosamunde Pilcher found an old Hermes typewriter in the attic which had been bought but never used by her father-in-law. She wrote whenever she found the time - short stories at first which were published in various magazines - and later novels. She still uses a manual typewriter and has never mastered either lap-top or computer.

In 1955 Rosamunde and Graham built their house near Dundee, and still live there. There is a large garden, with a tennis court and a small swimming pool, and plenty of space for children, grandchildren, friends, relatives and dogs and cats.

Rosamunde and Graham Pilcher today: "Marriage is like a job. A long, difficult job and both partners have to work harder than ever before."

106

PREVIOUS PAGES:
KILCHURN CASTLE NEAR LOCH AWE
(ARGYLLSHIRE)

We had to cross the main road, and follow a track which wound up between grass and heather, crossing and re-crossing a tumbling burn which passed under the road by means of a culvert and emptied itself into Elvie Loch. It had travelled from deep and high in the mountains, and the glen down which it ran, and the hills on either side, were all part of my grandmother's estate.   THE END OF SUMMER

FOLLOWING PAGES:
LOCH SHIEL, NEAR GLENFINNAN
(HIGHLANDS)

*T*he village was miniature. Oliver had never, in all the ten years of his life, seen such a tiny place. Six grey granite houses, a pub, an ancient church, a vicarage, and a little shop. Outside this was parked a rackety-looking truck, and somewhere a dog was barking, but apart from that, there did not seem to be anybody about.

THE BLUE BEDROOM

CROVIE IN THE
GRAMPIAN REGION
ON THE EAST COAST OF
SCOTLAND

110

*B*uilt of grey stone, long and low, turreted and gabled, it faced south, across a wide sloping lawn, to the loch. Too big, draughty and unheatable, shabby and constantly in need of repair, it was, nevertheless, his home, and the only place, in all his life, that he had ever really wanted to be.   WILD MOUNTAIN THYME

COUNTRY HOUSE ON THE
BANKS OF THE TWEED
IN THE BORDERS

CARVED AND INLAID WOOD IS
TYPICAL OF OLD SCOTTISH
FURNITURE

"Now, that's something that Benchoile has got and to spare. Security oozes out of the walls. I suppose it's something to do with the people who've lived in the house, and the way people live there now, as though nothing has changed in a hundred years."

WILD MOUNTAIN THYME   115

THE FURNITURE OF A
SCOTTISH COUNTRY HOUSE HAS BEEN
COLLECTED OVER GENERATIONS

*I*sobel led her visitor into the drawing-room, not with any intentions of grandeur but simply because it was full of sunlight, and the library and the kitchen, at this time of day, were inclined to be gloomy. The windows stood open, the room felt cool, and a mass of sweet peas, which Isobel had picked that morning, filled the air with their fragrance.   SEPTEMBER

DRAWING-ROOM OF A COUNTRY
HOUSE NEAR DORNOCH

*H*e got up and went to build up the fire, and to draw a chair close to the blaze, for Roddy. Roddy brought the drinks over, and handed John his, and then sank into the chair with what sounded like a sigh of relief. John remained standing, and the warmth of the flames crept up his back, and he realized that he was stiff and cold.

WILD MOUNTAIN THYME

TARTAN IS NOT JUST RESERVED FOR

KILTS

*S*he trod firmly down the flagged passage in the direction of the kitchen. Here the huge Aga, which never went out, rendered all comfortingly warm and cosy. Nancy sometimes thought, especially at this time of the year, that it was a pity they didn't all live in the kitchen. . . and any other family but theirs would probably have succumbed to the temptation and spent the entire winter there. THE SHELL SEEKERS

THE 'AULD ALLIANCE', THE SPECIAL
RELATIONSHIP BETWEEN SCOTLAND
AND FRANCE GOING BACK TO THE
12TH CENTURY HAS ALSO INFLUENCED
SCOTTISH CUISINE

*T*he library at Corriehill was a pleasant room, smaller than most of the other apartments, and smelled comfortably masculine — of pipe-smoke and wood-smoke, of old books and old dogs.

SEPTEMBER

THE WORKS OF THE FAMOUS
SCOTTISH POETS AND WRITERS ARE
PART OF EVERY PRIVATE LIBRARY: SIR
WALTER SCOTT - ONE OF ROSAMUNDE
PILCHER'S ANCESTORS -, ROBERT
BURNS, ROBERT LOUIS STEVENSON AS
WELL AS ROSAMUNDE PILCHER'S
FAVOURITE POET LOUIS MACNEICE

A floor creaked. Somewhere a door slammed shut. Croy. An old house with a heartbeat
all its own. Her home.

SEPTEMBER

GUN DOG CONSERVING ITS
ENERGY OUTSIDE THE
SHOOTING SEASON IN SCOTLAND

125

126

127

FOLLOWING PAGES:
BUACHAILLE ETIVE BEAG IN
GLENCOE (HIGHLANDS)

*F*ishing was special, because when you fished you thought about nothing else.

130   FLOWERS IN THE RAIN

She imagined the two young men in that world of endless moors and towering hills, bitter-cold northern seas, and deep, brown, fast-flowing rivers. They would fish together. Yes, it was a good decision that Danus had made. Fishing was said to be immensely therapeutic.

THE SHELL SEEKERS   131

Scotland is a country geared to the pleasures of menfolk, and there was always shooting to be got, grouse in the summer, and partridges and pheasants in the autumn and winter.

THE EMPTY HOUSE

For the first drive of the day, Rupert drew the top butt, which involved a climb not far short of mountaineering, trudging up a long, daunting slope through knee-high heather. It was another glorious August morning. The clear air was filled with the sound of bees and heather linties singing their hearts out, and the splash of small peat-stained burns tumbling down the hillside to join the river at the foot of the glen. From time to time they paused to cool their wrists and douse their faces in the ice-cold torrent, but, hot and sweaty, they finally made it, and the view from the summit made it all worthwhile.

COMING HOME

GROUSE SHOOTING IN THE
HIGHLANDS

133

				Grouse.	Ptarmigan.	Black Game.	Capercailzie.	Woodcock.	Snipe.	Plover.	Mallard.	Teal.	Various Duck.
Brought Forward.		Cluniemore & Duntanlich		331		12		4	2				
Aug 31st	D°. Sparden.	C J Kinloch & Self							3				
Sep 3rd	D°. Mid	Self.		1					2				
8th	D°. Mid	W A Malcolm & Self.		4									
14th	Duntanlich East Mid & West	L H Cox. A G Cox. G M Cox. G Robertson D Murray W A Malcolm Self		34									
5th	Cluniemore East Mid & West	L H Cox A G Cox G Robertson D Murray. W A Malcolm & Self		25					4				
19th	D°. Wood.	W A Malcolm & Self											
24th	D°. Banks.	D°.											
30th	Duntanlich. Mid.	Alf. W Cox & Self.											
23rd	Loch Broom.	W A Malcolm W Malcolm											
Oct 1st	Loch Broom.	Alf W Cox C M Boase											
3rd	Duntanlich West.	Alf W Cox & Self											
5th	Cluniemore (Riverside)												

Mrs Angus Steynton

At Home

For Katy

Friday, 16th September 1988

RSVP
Corriehill, Tullochard,
Relkirkshire

Dancing 10 P.M.

"You know what September's like." Isobel did know. The Scottish season, with a mass exodus from the south to the north for the grouse shooting. Every large house filled with house parties; dances, cricket matches, highland games, and every sort of social activity, all finally culminating in an exhausting week of hunt balls.   SEPTEMBER

Glenfreuchie was as much a success as Taddington had been a failure. The weather was perfect, the skies blue, and the hills purple with heather, and on their first day Athena cheerfully walked for miles, sat with Rupert in his butt, and kept her mouth shut when he told her to. The rest of the house party were friendly and informal, and Athena, with nothing expected of her, blossomed like a flower. At dinner that night, she wore a deep-blue gown that turned her eyes to sapphires, and all the men fell mildly in love with her. Rupert was filled with pride.   COMING HOME

SEPTEMBER IS THE SEASON OF HUNT
BALLS IN SCOTLAND: THE
INVITATIONS ARE ELEGANT AND THE
DRESS SHOULD SUIT THE OCCASION

*D*inner was over. They had sat, the six of them, around the candle-lit table, and eaten their way through Isobel's lovingly prepared celebratory meal. If she had not exactly killed a fatted calf, she had gone to great pains to produce a suitable feast. Cold soup, roast pheasant, crème brûlée, and a splendid Stilton, all washed down by the best wine that Archie could bring up from his father's depleted cellar.   SEPTEMBER

FESTIVE TABLE
FOR THE DINNER PRECEDING
THE BALL

RECIPES FROM ROSAMUNDE PILCHER'S KITCHEN

DRY MARTINI

4 parts London dry Gordons Gin to
1 part high-quality dry Vermouth.
Stir over ice.
Add a twist of lemon peel.

The chillier the tastier!

POTATO AND LEEK SOUP

12 oz. leeks
1 oz. butter or margarine
1 1/2 lb. potatoes
3 pints light stock
bouquet garni
salt and freshly milled black pepper
French bread
grated cheese

Makes about 3 3/4 pints:

Discard a third of the green tops from the leeks. Slice the remainder finely and wash thoroughly. Drain and place with 1 oz. butter in a large saucepan, cover and sauté 5 min.

Meanwhile peel and roughly dice the potato and add to the pan with the stock, *bouquet garni* and seasoning. Bring to the boil, reduce heat, cover and simmer for about 1 hr. until potatoes are soft. Discard *bouquet garni*.

Purée in an electric blender goblet or pass through a sieve.

Return to the pan, thin down with a little extra stock if you wish; adjust seasoning and serve with slices of French bread, topped with grated cheese and grilled. Garnish soup with chopped parsley.

PHEASANT THEODORA

named after Theodora Fitzgibbon who, some years ago, suggested this lovely idea of pheasants cooked with celery and bacon.

Serves 4
A brace of old pheasants
3 tablespoons soya oil
30 g (1 oz) rindless streaky bacon, diced
1 head celery, thickly sliced diagonally
1 tablespoon flour
430 ml (3/4 pt) pheasant or chicken stock
A *bouquet garni*
Salt and pepper
To complete
140 ml (1/4 pt) single cream
1 egg yolk, size 3

Set the oven at Gas Mark 4/180°C/350°F. Joint each pheasant into four. Heat the oil and butter in a large, heavy, flameproof casserole. Brown the pheasant joints a couple at a time, drain and remove.

Add the onion to the casserole and cook slowly until soft and golden. Add the bacon and celery and cook over medium heat until the bacon is golden brown and the celery softened. Stir in the flour, then the stock. Replace the joints, add the *bouquet garni*, season and bring to the boil. Cover and simmer gently in the oven for 1 to 1 1/2 hours until tender.

Remove the pheasant joints to a warm serving dish. Bring the sauce to a rapid boil for 3 to 5 minutes until reduced and slightly thickened. Mix the cream and egg yolk. Add to the sauce off the heat. Reheat gently, stirring constantly. Don't let the sauce boil or it will curdle. Taste and adjust the seasoning, then pour the sauce over the pheasant. Serve with noodles or rice.

CREME BRULEE AND RASPBERRIES

2 eggs
2 egg yolks
1 level tablespoon castor sugar
1/2 pint double cream
1/2 pint milk
Vanilla pod
Castor sugar
1 can raspberries (Baxter's, of course!)

Cream eggs, yolks and sugar thoroughly. Warm cream, milk and vanilla pod in a double saucepan then stir in the egg mixture. Cook gently until custard thickens, but stir constantly to prevent curdling. Strain into a fireproof dish and leave for 2–3 hours to set. Carefully spread an even layer of castor sugar over the custard. Put under the grill until sugar melts and turns brown. Chill thoroughly before serving with raspberries. Tap caramel sharply with a spoon to serve.

*T*he last bend, and the house was revealed in its full glory, towering up against the dark backdrop of the sky. It looked enormously impressive and proud.

Virginia said, "It must be feeling really good tonight."

"What must?"

"Corriehill. Like a monument. In memory of all the dinner parties, and wedding feasts and dances and balls that it must have known in the course of its history. And christenings. And funerals too, I suppose. But mostly parties." SEPTEMBER

144

"*W*hat would you like to drink?"
"Have you any whisky?"
"Of course. Grouse or Haig's?"
He could scarcely believe his luck. "Grouse!"
"Ice?"
"If you have some."   SEPTEMBER

"*It*'s a hell of a dance, isn't it?"

Startled, Noel looked around and saw the man who stood beside him, come, presumably,
to enjoy the spectacle, as he was.

He said, "It certainly is. What is it they're doing?"

"The Reel of the Fifty-first Highland Division."

"Never heard of it."

"It was devised in a German prison camp during the war."

"It looks extremely complicated."

"Well, why not? They had five and a half years to make the bloody thing up."

SEPTEMBER

FOLLOWING PAGES:
BRIDGE NEAR KILCHURN CASTLE ON
LOCH AWE (ARGYLLSHIRE)

145

Gibson took the road to Braemar by way of Tomintoul, driving south over the mountains and running down into the gold and sunlit valley of the Dee at about eleven o'clock. The river was in spate, deep and clear as brown glass, winding through fields and farmland and great stands of tall Scotch pine. THE END OF SUMMER

LOCHABER, GLEN GARRY (HIGHLANDS)

149

COUNTRYSIDE NEAR
SCADABAY
(ISLE OF HARRIS)

FLOWERING HEATHER
NEAR BALMORAL

"*I* love the colours of the moor because they remind me of the most beautiful tweed. All russets and purple, and larch-green and peat-brown. And I love the beautiful tweeds because they remind me of the moor. How clever people are to be able to emulate 150 nature so perfectly."

SEPTEMBER